ANIMAL COMMUNICATION

by Janet McDonnell

Created by

THE CHILD'S WORLD

Distributed by CHILDRENS PRESS®
Chicago, Illinois

The publisher wishes to thank the following for the use of their photographs: Ron Cohn/The Gorilla Foundation, 43, 45; David H. Funk, 27, 31; Jerry Hennen, 9; Robin Hunter/USFWS, 33; Dotte Larsen, 15, 17; L. David Mech/USFWS, 23; (D. Roby)/VIREO, 25; James P. Rowan, 37; Leonard Lee Rue III, 21; Ron Sanford, cover, 5, 11; Lynn M. Stone, 19; Tom J. Ulrich, 7; Doug Wechsler, 47.
The drawings throughout were made by Debra Ruggiero.
cover design by Kathryn Schoenick

Library of Congress Cataloging-in-Publication Data

McDonnell, Janet, 1962-
    Animal communication / by Janet McDonnell.
      p. cm. — (Amazing animal facts)
    Includes index.
    Summary: Examines forms of animal communication, including alarm signals, indications of territory, and mating rituals.
    ISBN 0-89565-513-6
    1. Animal communication—Juvenile literature.
[1. Animal communication.] I. Title. II. Series.
QL776.M38   1989
591.59—dc19   88-36643   CIP   AC

CHILDRENS PRESS HARDCOVER
EDITION ISBN 0-516-06388-X

CHILDRENS PRESS PAPERBACK
EDITION ISBN 0-516-46388-8

1 2 3 4 5 6 7 8 9 10 11 12 R 97 96 95 94 93 92 91 90 89

ANIMAL COMMUNICATION

Grateful appreciation is expressed to Mark Rosenthal, curator for the Lincoln Park Zoo, Chicago, for his assistance in insuring the accuracy of this book.

Can you guess what these baby birds are trying to tell their mother? Their constant chirping and wide-open, red mouths mean, "We're hungry!" The chicks are sending a message. That's called communication.

Just like people, animals have a lot to tell each other. And they do it in many, many ways. Every kind of animal has a special way of communicating. Some make noise, others make light, and some even make odors. Why do they go to all this trouble? Well, animals have very important things to tell each other. In fact, animals communicate to survive.

Steller's jay with chicks

Sound the Alarm!

When people see a fire, they sound a fire alarm. When animals sense danger, many of them also sound an alarm. One animal that has a very good alarm system is the prairie dog. Prairie dogs are not really dogs. They are rodents. They are called dogs because they can make a noise that sounds like a dog's bark. In fact, prairie dogs have a whole system of barks. Each has a different meaning.

When a prairie dog spots a hawk high overhead, it sounds the alarm. The prairie dog barks out a short, high-pitched note again and again very fast.

The others know just what that sound means—
HAWK! They dive into a hole for cover.

After some time, one or more prairie dogs peek
out of their holes. If the danger is gone, they will
give the loud, "all-clear" bark. To do this, they
stand up tall and throw their heads back. Then they
bark twice, very loudly. They come down on all
fours during the second bark. Sounds easy, right?
But it must not be. Sometimes, young prairie dogs
tip over backwards when they try the "all-clear"
bark.

Another animal that uses an alarm signal is the beaver. When a beaver senses an enemy approaching, it slaps its tail hard against the water. Sometimes the crack is so loud, it sounds like a gunshot!

If a beaver is in shallow water or on land when it hears the alarm, it will quickly swim to deep water. Most of the beaver's enemies cannot chase it there.

The alarm signal may help beavers in another way too. When a beaver slaps the alarm signal, water splashes everywhere. All that commotion may confuse the enemy and help the beaver make its escape.

An alarm signal means, "Look out! Danger!" Giving a warning is one way that animals help each other. There are other ways too.

For example, when a dolphin has been hurt or captured, it makes a whistling sound again and again. Just as your voice is different from everyone else's, no two dolphins have the exact same whistle.

A dolphin's whistle can be heard a very long distance away. When other dolphins hear it, they usually swim quickly to the sound. Sometimes, if the dolphin is hurt so badly that it cannot swim, one or more of its friends will push it to the surface so it can breathe. A helpful dolphin may swim under an injured one for as long as a week, going without food the whole time. After all, what are friends for?

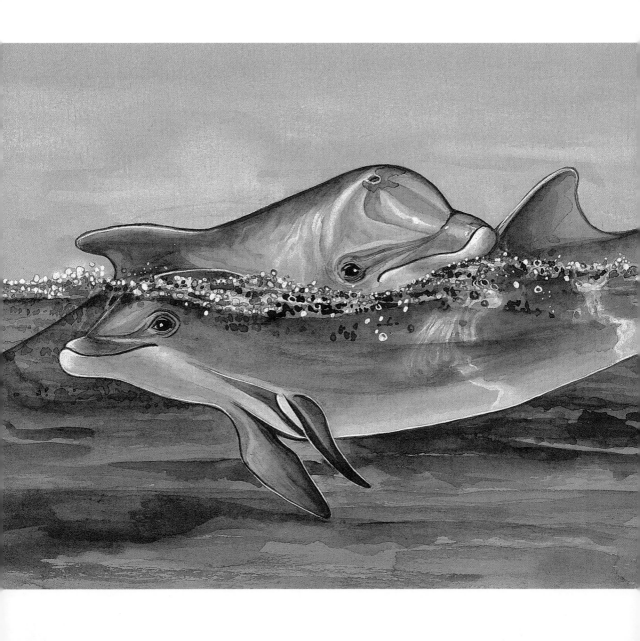

Whistling is only one sound that dolphins make. They can also click, squeal, and yelp. In fact, some people believe that these sounds make up a complicated dolphin language.

No one has "decoded" the language yet. But scientists are still trying. Maybe someday we will understand all the dolphin chatter that goes on in the sea!

All in the Family

Animals often make very good parents. They feed their babies, keep them warm, and watch over them carefully. And to be a good parent, animals have to communicate with their babies.

Penguins are one example of good parents. Penguins raise their young in "rookeries." Thousands and thousands of penguins live together in a rookery. When a parent penguin returns from the sea with food, it calls for its own chick. Now, all penguins may sound alike to humans, but not to penguins. When the hungry baby hears its parent, it answers the call and comes running for its food. The chick and its parent can tell each other's calls apart from the thousands of other noisy penguins.

Adelie penguin rookery

Even crocodiles can make good mothers. The female crocodile lays many eggs in a pit in the sand. After about three months, the babies are ready to hatch. They call for their mother to dig them out of the sand. When the mother hears the chirping sound, she hurries to the nest. She scrapes away the sand until she sees the eggs.

In an experiment, scientists played a tape of hatching crocodile babies to a female crocodile. She had laid some eggs, but they never hatched. Still, when she heard the tape, she rushed to the sound. Then she started digging. When the tape was turned off, she stopped digging.

Off My Property!

When an animal (usually male) claims an area for his own, it is called his territory. Animals can get very nasty when other members of their species invade their territory. To avoid fights, animals have many ways to tell others to "keep out." For instance, some animals leave odors to mark the boundaries.

The Thomson's gazelle (also called the tommy) is an antelope that lives in Africa. The male tommy keeps a small "harem" of four or five females within his territory. To keep other males away from his harem, the tommy builds a sort of "fence" of odors. In front of each eye, the tommy has a place that makes an odor. He rubs this spot on grasses and other things surrounding the territory. When other tommies smell the scent, they know to stay away —unless they want to fight!

Animals can also protect their territories with sound. People used to think that wolves only howled at the full moon. But that's not true. They howl to communicate many different things.

Wolves travel in packs. Sometimes when they are hunting, they stop to howl. This is to let other packs know, "Here we are!" Sometimes they hear an answer from wolves of another pack. That means "Look out! Don't get too close to our territory!" Wolves don't like to fight each other. By howling, they can avoid fights.

Birds also use sound to protect their "turf." The male bird warns other males to stay away by singing. He may sing from a tree in the center of his territory. Or he may fly from tree to tree around the edges of his territory and sing his song. It's hard to believe that such a pretty sound means, "Keep out, or else!"

But sometimes the male's song has another meaning too. To a female bird, it means, "Come to me." So at the same time the bird is warning away other males, he is trying to attract a mate.

Kirkland's warbler

Boy Meets Girl

Communication is very important to animals looking for mates. It may help a male "impress" a female. Or it may help the male and female find each other so they can breed.

For example, it isn't easy for male and female crickets to find each other in tall grass. So the male "sings" to attract the female. But the sound does not come from the cricket's mouth. He makes it by rubbing his wings together. One wing is like a comb. The other wing has a ridge on it. You can get the same kind of sound by dragging a pencil across the teeth of a comb.

Scientists have long believed that the female cricket follows the sound of the male's chirping to find him. To make sure that this is true, they experimented. First they put male and female crickets in separate cages. The cages were far apart from each other, but they were connected by telephone.

When the male crickets began chirping, the females headed straight for the telephone. They often climbed right up onto the receiver. It seems that was just the call they were waiting for!

Fireflies have a different way of attracting mates. They make no sound at all. Instead, they make light. On summer nights, you can sit on your front porch and watch what happens.

First the male flashes his light. The female sits on a stem of grass and answers by flashing back. The male keeps flashing, asking, "Where are you?" The female answers by blinking her light until he finds her.

There are many different kinds of fireflies. Some kinds are bigger than others. One type of large female firefly can trick smaller males. The tricky female blinks on and off for a male until he finds her. Then she eats him!

Humpback whales are much larger than fireflies and crickets. But they still may have a hard time finding each other in the deep, dark oceans.

To attract mates, the male humpbacks sing strange and beautiful songs. Their songs are made up of many different sounds. The whales moan, chirp, and cry. They even make a snoring sound!

Whales in different areas sing different songs, and the songs change slightly through the breeding season. It is believed that the dominant male in the group changes the song and the others follow.

You can hear these strange underwater love songs for yourself. Just ask your librarian to help you find the album called, *Songs of the Humpback Whale.*

Supper Time!

Another reason animals communicate is to tell others where to find food. Not all animals like to share. But some animals have to tell others about the food they find. Why? Because they need help carrying it.

For example, some types of ants have "scouts" that go out looking for food. When they find a big piece of food, they race back to the nest to get help. At the nest, the scouts feel the other ants with their antennae. Scientists think the scouts are passing along the smell of the food. In other words, the scouts' message is, "This is what it smells like. Go and get it!" And that's just what the other ants do.

But how do they know where to go? That's easy. The scouts have laid an "odor trail" on their way back to the nest. The other ants just follow the smell and march right to the food.

Honeybees have an even more amazing way of telling each other where the food is. They give directions! When a bee finds food, it flies back to the beehive to tell the other bees where it is. But the bee doesn't make a sound or a light. It does a dance! The other bees gather around and watch very carefully. Then they take off and find the food, even if it is miles away. Now those are good directions!

Scientists have watched the bees to find out how their dance works. They have learned that the bees do one kind of dance if the food is close by, and a different kind of dance when the food is far away. The "far-away" dance tells the bees if they should fly toward the sun or away from the sun.

While the bees dance, they also give off the scent of the flowers they've found. Then the other bees know what kind of flowers to look for.

Wagging dance (food far away)

Round dance (food nearby)

If I Could Talk to the Animals

By watching animals very carefully, people can learn to understand many of their messages. But some people want to do more than just watch. Did you ever wish you could talk to an animal, and that it could talk to you? Well, it is possible!

You may already know the amazing story of Koko the gorilla. A scientist named Francine Patterson has been working with Koko since Koko was a baby gorilla. Dr. Patterson has been teaching Koko to "speak" in American Sign Language (ASL for short). ASL is a language that uses hand signals and facial expressions for words. Talking with ASL is called signing. You may have seen deaf people signing.

Koko has been a good student. She knows over 500 signs! Using these signs, Koko can tell people how she feels and what she is thinking.

Koko likes to have Dr. Patterson read picture books to her. Sometimes Koko signs as she looks at the books. When she sees the angry mother in "The Three Little Kittens," Koko makes the sign for *mad*.

Koko likes cat books very much. So Dr. Patterson was not surprised when Koko asked for a pet kitten. She gave Koko a grey kitten that had no tail. Koko showed how clever she was when she named the kitten "All Ball."

Using ASL, Koko could tell everyone how she felt about her pet. "Koko love Ball," she signed, and, "Soft, good cat cat."

Sadly, All Ball was hit by a car and died. Later, Koko saw a picture of a cat that looked like All Ball. "Cry, sad, frown," she signed. But there is a happy ending. Koko has a new kitten which she named, "Lips Lipstick." To learn more about Koko, read *Koko's Kitten*, by Dr. Patterson.

Koko is not the only animal to learn to "speak" to humans. A chimp named Washoe was one of the first to learn to sign. She has been using ASL for many years. Scientists have even seen Washoe signing to another chimp!

Scientists are learning more and more about how animals communicate. And if you watch carefully, you may learn more too. At the zoo, in the wilderness, and even in your own backyard, you'll find animals communicating. Can you guess what they're saying?

Asiatic elephants greeting each other

INDEX